HOME MOVIE, NOWHERE

❉

HOME MOVIE, NOWHERE

✺

JULIA MADSEN

NEW MICHIGAN PRESS

TUCSON, ARIZONA

NEW MICHIGAN PRESS
DEPT OF ENGLISH, P. O. BOX 210067
UNIVERSITY OF ARIZONA
TUCSON, AZ 85721-0067

<http://newmichiganpress.com>

Orders and queries to <nmp@thediagram.com>.

ISBN 978-1-934832-81-3. FIRST PRINTING.

Design by Ander Monson.

Cover image: Photo 159976241 © Eddie Rodriquez |
Dreamstime.com

CONTENTS

Museum of Domestic Architecture   1

Home Movie, Nowhere   13

Bibliography   45

Acknowledgments   47

MUSEUM OF
DOMESTIC ARCHITECTURE

When the reel clicks over, a family gathers around the harvest table of a farmhouse located off a long stretch of highway. The sign says "Frytown" with an arrow pointing down the road and into the vanishing point, where the road turns to gravel. The vanishing point becomes a pupil and inside the pupil a semi-transparent mirror reflects a portrait.

Angle Road,* once part of a well-worn stagecoach line, now forms the forks by which we know our location in real space. It is a small breath of land, to be precise. It is both excision and exhumation, to be more precise. It is not unlike the pattern cutting of the prairie become grid, patchwork fields. The farmhouse floats on a plot of land just past the fork, a large and imposing clapboard structure when viewed from the road, but once inside one is immediately taken by its close confines. The bedrooms are all connected. Walls are thin. At your left is the laundry room, at your right, stairs to the basement, and in front of you is the mudroom. You already know what to do: slip off shoes. Hang jacket. There is a hook for every member of the family—brass handles engraved with initials. AMM. TNM. JMM. JNM. Every one in its place.

---

* Angle Road runs diagonally across a grid of square townships. The townships were established by the Land Ordinance of 1785, allowing for the purchasing and settling of land. According to Michael Martone, "[i]n Iowa the idea of the township was raised to the nth degree. The squares of the sections quilt the larger squares of townships that form the squares of counties. It is a joke in Iowa that there is only one diagonal road" (*Townships* 7-8). Our work resides on one side of that stern offshoot, inevitably tethered to its other.

The kitchen is narrow with a woven rug placed in center. The pantry has a long sliding door, rusted red and carved with names of former inhabitants, which my mother had taken off the side of the barn. Everything about the set design is rustic: in the dining room stands a knotted pine table and hutch filled with homespun wares over which natural light washes. You pause for a moment, glance out the paneled windows onto the lawn. It's almost afternoon. A rerun of *Gunsmoke* is playing from the living room, filling the void. It is like any other living room, with a television boxset, coffee table, and couches. You look at the small stained-glass window facing the road, just to the left of the television, then back to the television where a lonesome rider drives his horse across a vast expanse. The glass is old and wavy, making the landscape appear warped.

You take the stairs at the back wall of the living room lined with family photographs. It is like a gallery of the living and dead, still frames caught on photographic paper, moments which are not (so much) forgotten: grandmother standing in front of the farmhouse waving with one hand and shielding her face from sunlight with the other; father resting an elbow on a car door, one leg crossed over the other, holding a Pepsi; father as a child in a suit and tie; mother laughing and eating pie; the five of us standing in front of the cornfield at the golden hour, our heads backlit and electrified; myself and my sister, a portrait of us as small children captured in innocence as she puts a hand over mine.

Bedroom 1: A room intended as a nursery, with space only for a twin bed and television set. Angled ceiling, no wallpaper.

Bedroom 2: Larger room with two windows, one of which looks out on the road and the field beyond it spotted with cattle; a dresser and full-length mirror, bed, and open closet doors.

Bedroom 3: Darker and more shaded than the others, facing both front and side views of the home; a soft velveteen bedspread, dresser, and closet.

All bedrooms meet on a square landing at top of the stairs, each room a chamber, every thought echoing.

In the basement you hear a trickle of water drip from ceiling to floor. It is a zone of morbid curiosity and spiderwebs—shelter, too, from tornados and high winds, where you sit on the concrete floor or lean against wooden shelving, fiddle with the radio, "hello," a voice says, "can you hear me," but then static takes over. Like ghosts who roam these spaces, retreating into obscurity and white noise—but what should we want? To throw off silence? To leave? Don't ask me. I swallow fear until the obscene dark finds me lost and out of sorts. Which stairs are which? How to get out of the cave? First, you turn on the lights. The lightbulb is attached to a broken string (true). With each step the light flickers (true). The cat is sleeping on the ledge (true). Inside the hatch are stairs that once led to the basement (true). You step in a pool of water (false). There is a key on the ledge—take the key.

You walk upstairs and exit the backdoor, which is also the front, either or. This is one disorientation that allows for a different experience depending on which door you enter: if you open the door facing the road, the original before the addition was built, you will discover a loophole that takes you back to the family home as it once were, cast in living relief; but in doing so you also open possibility for other pasts to return, such that a cohabitation of histories emerges; and if you enter the door facing the gravel drive, you will find a house empty of characters yet still containing a resemblance of that former life, replete with all the home's old furnishings, untouched and unused for years as in a museum.

Above ground, on the acre-wide plot, there is a barn slouched to the side with a star above the loft's window, for good luck. You can see the star from the third bedroom, a focal point burned into memory, for I thought that looking at the star every night before bed would bring good sleep. It never did.* Now I am searching for those nights. And should they converge with what I already know, or will come to find, then will I finally resolve the pursuit? The other side can be seen through a pinhole in a dark room, the place where light enters, a star burning in the middle of the forehead. What shall I liken it to? An egress in the back of the mind, light dripping from a pinhole? In the back of the skull a door cracks open enough to know another room exists beyond its frame.

---

* I could hear sheep in the field yawning through the night, reminded of my own inability to sleep, staring at the ceiling like a blank scrim or screen. After some time a spider awakens from the cracks. A spider awakens from a sac filled with other sacs, the shadows of innumerable baby spiders. They crawl along the edge of that sleepless domicile just at the right of the fork.

Outside there is a summer kitchen, shed, garage, chicken coop, and corn silo. Relics of another time, all of them. The fence is barbed along the edges of the property that meet field: weeds poking through, wildflowers growing, rotting posts. "It helps keep out the rats," my father says by telephone, "hell," he says, "sometimes it don't." He calls himself a master trapper, having learned the proper way to do so after years of catching and skinning muskrats all along the banks of Big Slough Creek. He is on alert for any potential infestation from the edges of the field ("I used to make fifteen dollars for one pelt," he says, "I fell neck deep, true story into a beaver hole in dead of winter. Had to walk a half mile home"). I don't ask about the procedure of skinning a dead animal but understand. One creates distance from the thing that is held. There is blood on the hands, always—there is no getting beyond facts. And now, having walked back, you find yourself gazing across the expanse of fields and houses, spaced equally apart, running parallel to one another.

Is one house so different from the next, running parallel and squared off? There is a skeleton key rubbing rust into your palm, and you must catch your breath to walk in a such a vacuumed, airtight space—a profane gallery, a gallery of the living and dead (if, unlocking the door on the other side of the house, you enter—)

Unlocking the door, we have brought into existence the quaking and rattling of a harvest table in a farmhouse somewhere in the past. The door swings open. In walks a shadow in the shape of the grandmother, hunched in the form of a question. She will sit again. "Grandmother," I ask, "how have you been?" A daring question for one who has encountered nowhere and the nothing residing within it. She will turn to look at me with a cataracted eye as though she is looking through me, and without blinking will point toward the north where the cemetery hedges the road. Perhaps she has only been dormant for some time. Her exhumed breath will not frighten the animals, who sit and stare along. The dog does not bark. He knows the hand that fed him under the table all those years, but her fingernails have grown long and crooked. I ask, "when will I know if it is finished?" She blows out the candle. Smoke fills the screen. She leaves again in an unearthly gasp of wind.

HOME MOVIE,
NOWHERE

A woman and a man put their hands together like arrows pointed up toward some augury that will never come and when it doesn't, they forgive the augur. Why? Their lives are fraught with what it means to survive history. This is, after all, a dark valley of the mind, a pivot between present and past. Had you lived in another time, you would find the ancestors up all night, their faces flat and composed with loneliness. They are waiting. We glance into a mirror in the wake of a strange calmness and see an ancient face with ancient eyes looking out on the territory. All of this searching, yet we cannot gather our senses. All of this avowal buried below the grasses. My grandmother broods in a corner of thought, a rocking chair moving back and forth, back and forth. Were she unhappy she would cross her arms and fold her mouth or skin the flesh of an apple without a sound. She appears now as an image far and away, spitting out the seeds of that fruit.

Have you seen the black and white afterimage, a nip of whiskey lingering on the tongue? Have you found a way out? Whisper, I can only use my two eyes and something I have kept for a long long time. Whisper, mnemosyne.

Dear sister, do you whisper, then turn? A mirror reflection? A present given and taken away? Sister, I am so far up the branches and won't come back down. I will have been here for ages, on the brink of night. I will slink into a fold of memory, no, I will steal across the pastures like a steed, wandering and soulless, uncouth and barely alight, having shed the gown, having shed the skin of my skin, having known my way around here.

In the quiet focus of days I watched bales of hay change shade and shadow, the coming darkness I would always elicit and lean into while looking out. Even now I think of *foreboding* and how close it is to *forbidden*. I wanted to bite down on the flesh of a ripe fruit. The juices would trickle down my chin and breast and down my legs and become sticky. I looked at my shoulders in the mirror, bare and sticking out. I looked at my round face and hung the towel up to dry. I stole a beer from the fridge like cracking open a feeling of suppressed desire and drank it naked on the edge of the bed. I would make up my mind to drive to the State Theater* alone, taking in the cold of that brick relief, shivering with delight through the features. I gazed at the screen like a flat expanse or plateau on which to record a feeling so familiar I could only retrieve it by looking. I watched movies like they were a kind of pornography. I saw a man jerking off. I watched him wipe cum on the bottom of his seat. He never looked back once though he may have felt my eyes. I followed him out of the theater. I saw him get in his car and drive away while I drank the last of my Slurpee until I realized I was only sucking air. Brain freeze. Numb tongue. A red Firebird. *Yes, please.* But I didn't get to see his face.

---

*The oldest theater in the world, a curtain to another world, an escape. The watch's clockface glows and tells me time is almost up. But the movie is never over. The theater never closes. The ghosts of that theater remain in their seats, reemerging when the time is most appropriate. Georges Méliès** kept his work hidden in a cardboard box that was marked "look for historical value" with Sharpie, arriving some hundred years later when historian Michael Zahs would finally open it. Without Zahs we might never have recovered Méliès's lost work, which was buried under dust and subject to time. The theater itself has remained open since 1897, presided over by its original owners Frank and Indiana Brinton, to whom the lost films belonged.

> **The film director and illusionist, well-known for his innovative cinematic work at the turn of the century, including "stag" or pornographic films.

I played *Eyes Without a Face* when the house was empty and thought of the man at the movie theater. While I stared at the ceiling he took the palm of his hand and pressed it into my face, then put his fingers in my mouth, down my throat. He scratched my voice until I could hear static coming up from the floorboards, the television on low—or so I imagined. The spider says, "I've grown uncomfortable poking around in the back of my eye." She says, "we're going to start this a little different." She says, "the long road flattening out."

When farmers spread manure over fields the smell thickly covers every inch of land and insinuates itself inside the crooks of the house, and you are sure that the whole town has been released from the bowels of the gods who brought us here. The land is farmed by the Amish and Mennonite, and generations had gone by since followers of Noah Troyer* and others who came to proselytize the end days lived here. Until the crosswinds changed. At first there was an imperceptible shift, and then the fields fell silent, and cicadas began coughing up their dry call. It should have been a time of high harvest, but the corn was old and desiccated and rats emerged from fields to infest houses. They ate housecats and birds and nested between walls. Late at night you could hear them falling through the walls, but it is unknown how they got there. My father said he heard rats tumble from attic to basement. He said we needed a miracle. One morning three jars of honey appeared on our doorstep, but when my father found them he looked over to the neighbor's house and something darkened and changed in his face. He threw them away. We should have thought it an offering.

---

*Noah Troyer lived only a few miles north of Frytown and would issue prophecies from an unconscious or trance state while lying in bed. People came from great distances to hear his orations, and it was rumored that he could see things "'the natural eye cannot perceive'" (Harry H. Hiller, "The Sleeping Preachers" 22). He died by accident when a musket exploded and hit him in the eye. He was just trying to shoot and prepare chicken for the night. "'I must warn you that the time will come when the door will be shut and you will be cut off'" (Hiller 22). He believed in repentance before the final judgement. He said we should wash away all our sins. We wash them with mud in the creeks that have dried up and there the dead fish fumigate our senses. He wears a bandage over his left eye. His right eye has taken on the strain of the other, bulbous and bulging out of its socket. He walks along the dried-up beds behind a curtain of grasses. He is half-dead.

I was told the man who lived in the house parallel to ours across the field would never come out during the day on account of his private nature, but my sister swore she had seen him once with a beekeeper's mask over his face. I would sit on the front porch squinting to try and catch a glimpse. He became the subject of many myths and lore, including one my sister told about how he tried to poison the well as a child in an attempt to kill his neighbors. "Why didn't he like them?" I asked. "Because," she said, "they shot his dog on accident." She said, "now he holes himself up in that house, holding a shotgun whenever anyone comes up his steps." In a sense I could understand his fear of strangers. I would feel my heart racing whenever someone rang the doorbell and I was all alone and would run up the steps to my bedroom and peak out the curtains to see who it was. Could only close my eyes and hope the ringing would stop.

Here on the land of the Sauk and Meskwaki we admonish the dust of our knowledge while the sleeping preacher prophecies collapse. He is an outsider, an intruder from some unknown and far off place. He will pretend to understand the ways of people who live here, their steadfast desires, their hope in a god who has not lost sight. He preaches from a throne of bedsheets. He has come back to tell us what we need. He speaks always of the wide road and narrow road and tells us to watch for snakes that lie in wait in stagnant pools of poison water. When he replaces his bandage, the blood and pus of days oozes and his face becomes colorless. He is ghastly with the meaning of the word that implies a fearful, horrid smile, his teeth are fallen out, and he gums the rough end of a muddy stick while looking down on his own gravestone which has been effaced by a hundred years of rain and wind. He is happy and not happy to find his corpse dug up from the depths. He has come back to fulfil a premonition. When he cracks a smile, you know time is almost up.

There is a telephone booth on the side of the road in case of emergency, on the corner in front of Herm's old house which has fallen now into vacancy.* If I were to call from that booth, would he answer from a beyond? Would I receive the message? Or would the memory vanish, recollected only in the archive of a text where his visage has been darkened and pixelated by photocopy?†

You lie awake wondering what the Amish do at night, admiring their way of life, their belief in god and eternity. If you were like them you could, you tell yourself, read books under the light of an oil lamp, or keep yourself busy making bread. You would eat each morsel reverently and with the appetite of a thousand men. Your days would stretch on into the vanishing point, after which you are not certain what happens. You have been told the angels will be playing their Aeolian harps and singing with vocal chords unknown and unmatched by any mortal. What if they sing too sweet? What if their voices infuriate me, so that I take up the mirror and smash it?

---

*Years later I will take myself to that house and stand on the edge of the ragged lawn, looking into the windows for what I do not know, then drive to the bar off the corner of Orville Yoder and Black Diamond where I place a quarter on the jukebox and whittle time away remembering how his ghost would appear in the doorway of that bar, but we never saw him again. Should we forget our neighbors and the questions they unravel before us? And all the meals we ate together in the middle of a snowstorm in late winter, him having taken caution just to reach our warm house? There would be wine flowing, a celebration just for the living. Mother would be there, serving up anything you could think. I would not like to think of him in the fluorescent hospital any more than I would like to think of the grave now marking his loss in Frytown's cemetery. Zahs tells us that "the word cemetery started about the same time Washington County** did. It means a dormitory where people are sleeping. It doesn't have anything to do with death or burial ... but about that same time people quit dying. They started passing away. Crossing the river. Buying the farm. Kicking the bucket. But we started sleeping in a cemetery called the dormitory the same time we quit dying" (*Saving Brinton*). At least he is safe there, in bed, at the right of his father. And to return to his picture as a singular remnant—where he is young, unknowing, unsunk into the depth. I know that to remember him here is the very thing that kills a man.

**Frytown exists on the boundary-edge between Johnson and Washington Counties, marking the spot between central and southern Iowa. On one side is the city; on the other, small towns and endless countryside. Frytown is a bedroom community of Kalona which resides in Washington County. When the Burlington, Cedar Rapids, and Northern Railway was built through Kalona in 1879, the stagecoach line to Frytown abruptly ended, and the town has since staggered but remained. When the railway closed, Kalona faced total dissolution, but it hasn't dissolved, not yet, and at night if you listen closely you can still hear the echoes of the late train.

†I see his picture in the only piece of literature on this town—a self-published volume archiving the passage years from 1854-1984. He stands with his brother and father in front of the auto repair shop. I look back at him, through him. I ask a question. I wait for the message in the middle of the road.

After spending some time here you learn. People come and go or they never leave, they never even come. You find there is a way of hiding out. You make do passing time. You get up every morning to work at the hardware store then go to school then back to the hardware store. You wait to leave, watching the second hand stutter past ten o'clock. You find yourself driving to the apartment complex of the guy who manages the front end. He says he wants to watch 300 but really wants to lie down on the bed with his arms crossed behind his head after taking a hit. This doesn't happen. He is somewhat awkward about the whole thing. You sit on the couch and watch the entire movie in near silence. How many times have we seen this one before? Somehow he ends up at your house, in your bedroom. Your parents are sleeping. His eyes are red and when you walk down the hallway to the bathroom it seems to take a lifetime. Earlier he told you about the man in the bathroom crying out about how good it felt to take a piss. This was one of those kinds of pisses. You smell like shit and your eyeliner is smeared. You smile and let it hang there, half-finished.

I was reading *In Cold Blood* before bed and felt a tempered suspense rising in the voice and in the breast. How something so terrible could happen to as decent of a man as Herb Clutter. He reminded me of my father, polite and generous, though I might add that we never knew the kind of prosperity as the Clutters. My father worked as a mechanic at a gas station before he quit because his boss had started to torment him in small ways— leaving mice out for him to find, pissing in Mountain Dew bottles, etc. I only caught parts of the story here and there from my sister who worked the cash register after school. She said the boss was a drunk who left to drink with his friends every day at the corner bar called Mummie's. Or when she told me, and dare not repeat, that she found a diary hidden inside a binder below the desk. It was written by one of the boss's friends, and amounted to crude and lurid descriptions of every employee who worked there— all written while the boss was gone on vacation, she said, and intended for his entertainment upon return—including entries on the boss's own son, who had been described as masturbating behind the register while the friend watched.

After the rats moved in, the houses along Main Street grew further and further apart. Some people did not want to step foot outside on account of what Noah called a plague. He said god was an imprecation and said we ought to leave our houses and farms and abandon what was not ours. He said we no longer belonged here any better than the rats that had grown fat with sweetbreads and scraps of food left over in pantries, and one night at the end of equinox I looked up and admit to you now, reader, that I saw a harvest sky full of blood, I saw a tinge that no one should recollect. What if our poison and trappings did not chase out the rats? I prayed though I no longer believed in prayer, I tried to speak with my dead grandmother under the harvest sky.

Grandmother did not answer. She had already escaped down that gravel road, no need to travel back to forsaken ground. There was corn everywhere—piles stacked like corpses against barns and outhouses and sheds. Noah and his followers were planning to hold a meeting at the auction house in the windless heart of town. There were flyers nailed to the sides of buildings, taped to screen doors, they would knock twice—and were gone. Many people started to get sick with unknown ailments, and others were worried about an entire season's worth of crop gone to dust. I went to the auction house to catch sight of a scene I might find only in the movies. When Noah's eyes rolled into the back of his head, everyone let out a gasp. The loose meat hamburgers we grasped in our hands turned to maggots, and a chill air descended from the rafters. The auctioneer called for attention with his mallet. "We have assembled ourselves," he said in a voice more trembling than certain, but before he could finish we saw flies rise from maggots roiling in sawdust, and bull snakes approach from the corners of the room.

A bed was placed in the center of the auction house's concrete floor. Noah spoke his prophecies from under a pillow, lying there with bloated gut, sweating from every pore. He told us the dead would come again and cracked a smile. He said, "you have not lived long enough to tell the time of day." He said, "we will remember what they came for" and many other sordid babblings rising up from the gut. His veins grew red and engorged, and he shook in the frenzy of a fever, thrashing to and fro atop a bed laid out by ungodly knowledge.

I went home that night with a feeling of perdition and a restless soul. I stared at the only photograph of my grandmother as a child—dug up from the basement where I spent time with her old belongings, which she had kept hoarded in garages and outbuildings, overflowing her house. She fades out of frame. Her father is touching her shoulder—a man whose silhouette could only cast darkness over the sun. She said, "it happened to all of us." She said, "it was that, or worse." I am with her now once again, reaching out a hand to clasp her breath as it rises, falls. Her long floral nightgown faded under lamplight. Her three bottom teeth sunken and stained. How did we intend to deal with uncertainty when we were ourselves running barefoot toward abandon? How did she speak, a soft creak of the voice, a hint of the ghost beneath it?

Her father lived a hundred and four years, a man of unholy desires of the flesh and grandmother called him a wretch and spit on his grave. He was an alcoholic and lived in poverty in the hills of Missouri, which we pronounced "misery," until he died. "He should have known," she said, and drifted away to a place I cannot imagine. "For a time, I was his favorite," she said. I wince. I fall back. I become the corpse locked in a grave and cannot, for the life of me, find a way out. I call. I don't call. My voice mixes with the muddied ground and my flesh softens into loam. This is death's trapdoor. This is quicksand. This is the only exit.

Perhaps you would like to see a film by Georges Méliès projected onto the scene—"Une séance de prestidigitation"—or perhaps you will think all of this an impossibility, a misapprehension. But I will have been there, I will have known. There is smoke filling the screen, a dove flown from the cuff of a sleeve. There is the body of my grandmother, placed in a pine box where she disappears forever. I hear jangling like a key in the back of the skull and am brought back.

It is almost midnight here. The dissolving projector plays the same film on repeat, but the order of images changes each with each. Méliès would shudder to think we're watching the film alone. He would like to sit with us in a cool, darkened room like ghosts haunting a cave, growing more and more transparent. Is death a part of the blank background? Will it wait for us to fall asleep? Méliès takes us by the hand through a curtain to the other side.

.

On the darkened side of the mirror to the left of the fork the neighbor tended his beehives. He became a trace of that other side, living a double life—he was, inevitably, the father, keeper of night. As a child I would watch *Ulee's Gold* on repeat, a movie about a beekeeper who tries to keep his family together in rural Florida, whose granddaughters always reminded me of myself and my sister—the youngest not yet a teenager, the oldest almost eighteen, wanting only to get away from the place so she is leaving all the time and causing a scene, which is how I felt about my sister. But Ulee continues to tend his flock—though he is stern, saddened, pinched in the face—having put up with his son's imprisonment and daughter-in-law's addiction, having taken care of the bees—he even looks like the farmer from the American Gothic painting. On his plot of land the neighbor lifts the top off a wooden box, blows smoke, then takes the honeycomb from its place, turning it over to look at the work they have done. Is time a slow, viscous fluid in which we are caught? Like a fly in candlewax? "We don't ask outsiders for help," Ulee says. "We don't need the whole damn world knowing what's going on in our house."

These days my sister lives in a loophole where the same images play on repeat. I wonder what she sees, what she doesn't see. I could tell you about addiction, I could tell you about guilt and shame—how when we lived in that house she would say, "I wish I could get drunk so I could tell all of you how I really feel." Like a prescient insight, knowing that things haven't changed so much. I wonder about my own part, though I have been told not to wonder, so I wander in and out of memories as one might a fugue state. I would tell her that I, too, am guilty, but have never known for what. Was it isolation? The confines of that house? What was I afraid they might find out?

Maybe the neighbor was a projection of an inner desire for privacy, a manifestation of childhood anxiety, what we all wanted but couldn't find the words to say. He lived in solitude and seclusion, tending nightly to his bees while everyone else was sleeping. He was fascinating for the very fact of existing *outside*—like on another plane of existence, away from the all-surveilling eye of a small town in the middle of the middle of the Heartland. I look over to his house across the field. A voice crackles through static on the porch radio. "Hello," the voice says, knowing someone, anyone, can hear.

Sometimes I thought I could still hear the late train hissing past Kalona, having tunneled the underworld and crossed the Mississippi like the River of Styx. There the ancestors were waiting like a collection of secrets. The words didn't come in clear; I had to attune them through practice and diligence if I wanted to hear anything. Like Orpheus bent over the radio, I was afraid to look back and afraid to look forward. I ate a pomegranate whole and spit out the seeds. I was alone. I was sufferable. There was a choice to be made, and many choices that followed.

I tried to write myself out of a place and found myself digging deeper. In *root* I found a place to return to, a depth we must plumb, the radix from whence we come and the unanalyzable etymon which precludes our powers to say so. And many other things at once, branching off like free intensities. I imagined that my internal nature was beginning to mirror the fields around me, which by now had undergone several burnings so that they might return richer and more fertile. I stuck my hands into soil all the way up to the elbow. I confided in the soil, felt worms crawl and still kept digging deeper and deeper. There are those hallowed moments hollowed of sound where only the nothing speaks.

Before bed my father used to tell me a story about a woman with a yellow ribbon. There was a man way back in old times, he would say, the captain of a merchant ship who met a seamstress and she always wore a dress with a ribbon around her neck. One day after so long he asks her why she always wears the ribbon. "Why don't you take it off?" he asks. "You'll be sorry if I do, so I wont," she says. As time goes on, he gets more insistent. Every night at dinner he asks her why she won't take it off and she always replies, "you'll be sorry if I do, so I wont." He comes up with a plan. He waits until the middle of the night when she is asleep. He tiptoes quietly to her sewing basket and gets out a pair of scissors, then holds the scissors up to the ribbon and snip goes the scissors and snap goes her head and it rolls over into the moonlight as she wails tearfully, "I told you you'd be sorry." I imagine that gleaming double-edge cutting the ribbon binding life and death, her head rolling endlessly, disembodied, over hills and floating across the river conducting souls from one world to the next.

Maybe Noah, too, was a manifestation, a phantom capable of making any illusion appear real, full of trickery and deception— and also luck. It is no wonder he would play magic lantern shows every Saturday night at the old Frank Pierce Entertaining Company building on the furthest edge of town. He would run his cowboy shows backward and forward, charging five dollars to watch. Was he not the star of his show? His well-known prophecies had stopped come winter, when rats tunneled their way out of walls and back into fields where they froze, and so too did Noah, who packed up his show and left town unbeknownst to his followers. I think of him now, wandering the fields in a trance, standing at the center of the crosswinds with the ecstasy of having lived again.

Today another family lives in that farmhouse. After a tornado carved through town, we thought we would burn down the house and build anew given structural issues brought on by vacuum-like winds. A Mennonite family offered to move it a couple miles down the road so they could live in it. My mother said the move took hours, and many rat skulls tumbled out of those walls. I visited that home years later, walking through rooms from the perspective of an outsider, as though I had never lived there, as though I were only a visitor, an intruder, which I was. When I pulled up my car in the gravel drive, a circle of children gathered around, wanting to show off their pets and take me inside to eat ice cream. I did. Their mother led me through the home, showing me their rooms and taking me into the basement, which to my astonishment was bigger and more inhabitable than ours had been—but near the crack in the window I saw a spider enshrouding a fly in its web.

I am reminded of a scene in *Children of the Corn* when the two main characters, Burt and Vicky, are driving the backroads of rural Nebraska and find themselves going through a maze of cornfields. They keep driving further into fields, and the children are watching, taunting from a distance. The children, too, want to escape but cannot. The enduring image is of a suitcase streaked with blood, hidden among cornstalks—for the children are inheritors of nothing and nowhere. What's in the suitcase? What sins of the father are the children paying for? What will they sacrifice? You already know. You've known all along. This is the long road cutting across distances, at once a maze and straight story, and the only way out is by having gone through.

BIBLIOGRAPHY

Hiller, Harry H. "The Sleeping Preachers: An Historical Study of the Role of Charisma in Amish Society." *Pennsylvania Folklife*, vol. 18, no. 2, winter 1968-1969, pp. 19-32.

Martone, Michael, editor. *Townships*. University of Iowa Press, 1992.

Saving Brinton. Directed by Tommy Haines and Andrew Sherburne, starring Michael Zahs, Barn Owl Pictures, 2017.

ACKNOWLEDGMENTS

A portion of this manuscript was originally published in *Burning House Press*. Thank you to the editors.

JULIA MADSEN is a first-gen writer, scholar, and educator. She earned an MFA in Literary Arts from Brown University and a PHD in English/Creative Writing from the University of Denver. Her first book of poetry, *The Boneyard, The Birth Manual, A Burial: Investigations into the Heartland*, was published in 2018 by Trembling Pillow Press.

✤

COLOPHON

Text is set in a digital version of Jenson, designed by Robert Slimbach in 1996, and based on the work of punchcutter, printer, and publisher Nicolas Jenson. The titles here are in Futura.

✢

NEW MICHIGAN PRESS, based in Tucson, Arizona, prints poetry and prose chapbooks, especially work that transcends traditional genre. Together with DIAGRAM, NMP sponsors a yearly chapbook competition.

DIAGRAM, a journal of text, art, and schematic, is published bimonthly at THEDIAGRAM.COM. Periodic print anthologies are available from the New Michigan Press at NEWMICHIGANPRESS.COM.

www.ingramcontent.com/pod-product-compliance
Lightning Source LLC
Chambersburg PA
CBHW020810130626
46554CB00006B/2369